IMAGES
of America

ROCKY MOUNT
AND NASH COUNTY

IMAGES
of America

ROCKY MOUNT
AND NASH COUNTY

Monika S. Fleming

ARCADIA
PUBLISHING

Published by Arcadia Publishing
Charleston, South Carolina

Printed in the United States of America

Library of Congress Catalog Card Number: 98-87447

For all general information contact Arcadia Publishing at:
Telephone 843-853-2070
Fax 843-853-0044
E-mail sales@arcadiapublishing.com
For customer service and orders:
Toll-Free 1-888-313-2665

Visit us on the Internet at www.arcadiapublishing.com

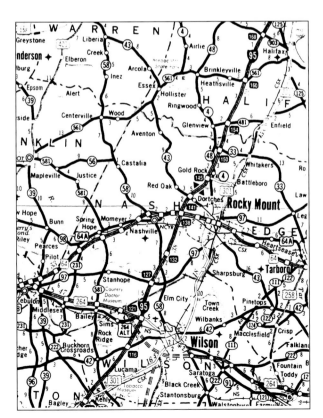

Located in northeastern North Carolina, Nash County is the transition area between the hilly piedmont and the flat coastal plains. Elevation in the county rises from east to west moving from 121 feet near Rocky Mount to over 300 feet at Castalia. Covering over 552 square miles, the county is bisected by Interstate 95 and Highway 64 and is midway between New York and Florida. (Courtesy of North Carolina Department of Transportation.)

CONTENTS

ACKNOWLEDGMENTS

Collecting photos for this volume took time and effort and would not have been successful without the help of individuals who were committed to this project. Photos were gathered from both individuals and organizations. All photos are credited after the captions with the name of the person or organization that contributed them.

Individuals who contributed to this work include JoAnne Crowe, Linda Journigan Faulkner, Sullivan and Dorothy Fisher, Connie Gorham, Fred and Hortense Hicks, the Richard Journigan family, James Marrow, Carolyn Moore, Ellen Faulkner Moore, Michael O'Brien, Jane and John Saunders, Dorothy Skinner, Elizabeth Tippett, and Tim Valentine. Their photographs are identified by their last names in parentheses.

Organizations included the following: Tom Smith at Bob Melton's, Susan Reese and the staff at Braswell Memorial Library (BML), John Kinchelow and Julia Cherry at Bullucks, Carolyn Bissitte at the County Doctor Museum (CDM), Julie Brown of First Baptist Church (FBC), Brenda Wright at Nash General Hospital (NGH), Sharon Outlaw of the Nash-Rocky Mount School System (NRMS), Hiriam Perkinson at Nash Community College (NCC), Jerry Jackson at the Rocky Mount Arts Center (RMAC), Joyce Dickens and staff at Rocky Mount Edgecombe Community Development Corporation at Harambee Square (RMECDC), and Kathy Winslow and the library staff at Wesleyan College (NCWC).

Several people contributed information for this volume or helped gather and prepare material. They include the staffs at Office Depot and Quick Print in Rocky Mount, Steve Henderson at WRQM, Patty Collins, Dick Stallings, Bruce McRoy, Betsy Fuller in Nashville, Anita Whitesell and Kenneth Murcheison of the *Spring Hope Enterprise,* and members of the ECC writers group Gladys Capel, Steve Pavelsky, and Carol Mehlie. I cannot overlook the vast information obtained from Dr. Margaret Battle, the historian of Rocky Mount and Nash County, followed by the research of Helen and Joseph Watson, and many others in the Nash County Historical Society.

I would like to express special appreciation to these archivists and researchers: Steve Massengill and Earl Iames at the North Carolina Division of Archives and History (NCDAH), and Mary Boccaccio at the Special Collections of East Carolina University (ECUSC).

Two people went beyond normal efforts, and without them much of this book would not have been possible. First to thank is David Chicelli at Barringer Studio, who shared countless photos from the files of Bugs Barringer. Many of the photographs in this volume were by Bugs Barringer or Charlie Killebrew, a photographer for the *Evening Telegram* for over 30 years. Both Bugs and Charlie preserved the images of Nash County life. Second to thank is Gretchen Journigan, a former student who made dozens of calls to friends and neighbors in northern Nash County and collected photos under a tight schedule. Without her, Red Oak, Aventon, and Hillardston could not have been represented.

Resources included clipping files at area libraries from back issues of the *Nashville Graphic, Rocky Mount Telegram,* and *Spring Hope Enterprise.* Earlier historical works include *Rocky Mount NC Centennial Commemorative Book (1867–1967),* Barringer, Barringer, and Chesson's 1977 *Pictorial History of Rocky Mount,* and *By Faith & Heritage Are We Joined—Nash County Historical Notes* (1976). Some biographical information came from *Dictionary of North Carolina Biography,* edited by William Powell, and some of the architectural information came from *A Guide to Historic Architecture of Eastern North Carolina* by Bishir and Southern (1996).

Finally, thanks to my brother-in-law, Kevin Fleming, who helped to gather and date photographs, and to my husband, Martin, for his support, his suggestions, and errands that helped complete this book.

Tar River Falls was the site of the Rocky Mount Mills, which gave birth to the community in 1818. The natural landscape of the falls provided the power source for the second oldest mill in North Carolina. The bridge and falls used to be the dividing line between Nash and Edgecombe County until the line was moved east in 1871. (ECUSC.)

INTRODUCTION

Located in northeastern North Carolina, Nash County is separated from Halifax County by Fishing Creek to the north, from Johnston County by Moccasin Creek on the south, and from Edgecombe County by the railroad on the east. The western border is a man-made imaginary line dividing Nash from Franklin County. The Tar River winds through the county with a large reservoir in the southeast. Numerous creeks, such as Toisnot Creek and Beaverdam Creek in the south, Peachtree Creek in the northwest, Swift Creek in the northeast, and Sapony and Stoney Creek in central Nash, supply water and powered the many mills that spurred settlement.

Nash County's location on the fall line between the piedmont and the coastal plains drew many settlers in the eighteenth century. Some communities were settled in the 1740s, when Nash was part of Edgecombe County. As the population increased, Edgecombe was divided several times to form new counties. During the turmoil of the American Revolution, citizens in the far western areas of Edgecombe found it difficult to get to the county seat of Tarboro to conduct business. When the provincial congress met that fall in North Carolina, Nathan Boddie proposed that Edgecombe be split and a new county formed. The county was named Nash to honor North Carolinian General Francis Nash, who was killed at the battle of Germantown while fighting for American independence. Before the war was over, British General Cornwallis marched through Nash County on his way to Yorktown, and a small skirmish was fought along Fishing Creek between local militia and the British. When the first national census was taken in 1790, the population of Nash County totaled over 7,300.

Several communities would grow up along the stagecoach routes, which crossed the county. The north-south road, known as the Halifax route, was the impetus for Dortches in the 1780s. Dortches evolved from the Dortch House, which was remodeled in 1810. Other families who settled along this road included Griffin, Ellen, Gay, Coley, Proctor, Vick, and Bunn. The Ricks family would operate a tavern along this route in the area that becomes Red Oak. The Tarboro-Raleigh route ran east-west in southern Nash County along what is now Highway 97, and the

Stanhope community developed at a stop on this road. In the northern part of the county, the stagecoach from Halifax to Raleigh led to the taverns and eventually to the communities of Hilliardston and Castalia.

The first few decades in the new county witnessed residents settling near rivers and creeks, often building gristmills. In 1818, three adventuresome businessmen invested to build the second cotton mill in the state at the Falls of the Tar River, which was then in Edgecombe County. Half a century later, the county line moved east and Rocky Mount Mills became part of Nash County.

The biggest change to Nash County occurred between 1830 and 1840, when the Wilmington to Weldon railroad was completed. The first train went through to Weldon on March 9, 1840, after construction reached Rocky Mount in 1839 from Goldsboro. The railroad would shape the county with spur lines forming more communities, and the repair shops would result in a population burst at the end of the century.

The county seat of Nashville was thriving by mid-century with numerous merchants. Several private academies grew, as citizens wanted their children educated before public schools were available. Most residents were farmers on the eve of the Civil War, when the county population reached over 11,600. Approximately 42% of the population were African Americans.

Over a thousand men in Nash County would serve in five different companies in the Confederate Army. Several families contributed large numbers of soldiers. The Joyners sent 29 men; 7 died on the battlefield, and 3 others were wounded. The Griffin and the Strickland families each sent 20 men to war. Nash County men were at the first battle in June 1861 at Bethel Church, Virginia, and they were also in many major battles with the Army of Northern Virginia, including Gettysburg. The total casualties of Nash County, according to a book by Captain John Thorpe, were 65 men killed and over 100 wounded.

The war came to Rocky Mount in July 1863 when the Union forces led by Major Jacobs raided the Rocky Mount Mills and the railroad depot. After evacuating the mill, the Yankees burned it down and captured a train before destroying the railroad bridge and part of the tracks. Bellamy's Mill at Fishing Creek was converted to a factory to produce caps and uniforms.

After the war, Rocky Mount had grown enough to become incorporated in 1867. Then in 1871, under disputed circumstances, the county line between Nash and Edgecombe was moved over a mile from the river at the falls to the railroad. When the Atlantic Coastline railroad set up its repair shops in Rocky Mount in 1899, the population grew from less than 900 to over 3,000, and by 1920, the population was over 12,000. Nash County was also growing, with the total population over 40,000. By the 1950s, Rocky Mount was the largest bright-leaf tobacco market in the world.

Today, Rocky Mount has over 55,000 residents, and Nash County has over 83,000. The county is still active in agriculture, producing sweet potatoes, corn, tobacco, cotton, and peanuts. Livestock includes beef and dairy cattle, swine, and poultry farms. Even with agriculture, diverse industry and manufacturing in Nash County produces pharmaceuticals, diesel engines, textiles, jet engine controls, and hardware.

General Marquis de Lafayette toured America in 1825 and visited Nash County. Donaldson was one of the original owners of Rocky Mount Mills, having moved to the area from Edenton around 1816. In 1828, Donaldson sold his interest in the mills to the Battle family and relocated to Fayetteville, where he purchased the Fayetteville Mill at Cross Creek. This sign is located between Peachtree Street and Falls Road. (Barringer.)

One

Nashville and Central Nash County

The original name of the Nashville community was Nash Court House. In 1805, the post office began with John Lewis as the first postmaster. Early county commissioners were George Boddie, Hon. H. Drake, William Burt, Nicholas Drake, and Henry Blount. The General Assembly designated Nashville the county seat in 1815, and the town incorporated in 1823. An early store was Peters and Watson. Brothers Brian H. and William G. Freeman operated one of the largest stores in Nashville called Freeman and Freeman. The store sold brandy, silk, lace, and hardware items. The first church was the Methodist church established in 1812. The Nashville Male Academy opened in 1827, but public schools did not open until 1844. A railroad line came to Nashville in 1888. P.A. and Laura Richardson established a funeral home for African Americans. Richardson was a successful businessman, and a Nashville housing complex is named after the couple. In 1900, Nashville had a population of just under 500, and by 1910, it was over 750. Today, the population is almost 4,000, making it the second largest town in Nash County. Residents read the weekly *Nashville Graphic*. The former Baptist church built in 1914 has been converted into the Nash County Cultural Arts Center on Washington Street.

Other communities in central Nash County include Castalia, Corinth, Easonburg, Piney Grove, Peachtree, and Taylor's Cross Roads. Castalia still has an old-fashioned Fourth of July parade each summer.

The first courthouse burned in 1833 and was replaced by a brick building. In 1921, Rocky Mount architect John C. Stout designed the current courthouse in a colonial revival style. Located on West Washington Street, the Nash County Courthouse sits in the center of the business district. (NCDAH.)

9

Nashville residents line up along Washington Street for the annual Harvest Festival. Businesses in the 1940s included the Nash Theater, Nashville Dry Cleaners, and L.R. Bass & Brothers. In 1905, P.A. Richardson had a barbershop, and J.D. Barnes was the undertaker. The county seat boasted Nashville Collegiate Institute and Oak Level High School. S.R. Hilliard operated Hilliard Hotel, M.E. Collins ran the Collins Boarding House, and Mrs. M.C. Brake owned the other boardinghouse. J.T. Strickland and James P. Battle provided medical services, and T.T. Ross was the town dentist. General stores included Arrington-Bissett Co., Brooks Son & Co., Griffin & Ward, J.D. Winstead and Co., M.C. Yarboro & Co., and F.B. Cooper Co. Wallace Batchelor managed the livery stable. The town also had three sawmills and a shuttle factory. (NCDAH.)

The third annual Harvest Festival was held in the late 1940s. The Future Homemakers and majorettes are marching down West Washington Street. Businesses include Ward Drug Co., Batchelor Freeman Shoes, and Nashville Seed Co. Ward Drugs featured a soda fountain and is still in operation. (NCDAH.)

Pope's Five and Dime occupies the Nash Supply Company building, constructed in 1912. The company was incorporated under that name in 1905 after operating as V.B. Batchelors since the late nineteenth century. (NCDAH.)

Businessman George Bissette built this house in the residential section of East Washington Street in Nashville. This Queen Anne house was completed in 1898 and had the town's first ceramic bathtub. Later, Bissette hired architect John C. Stout of Rocky Mount to build the Bissette-Cooley house, which became the home of Congressman Harold Cooley. (NCDAH.)

Located in Castalia, the Billy Lou Arrington house was built in 1874 and may be the oldest standing home in the community. Other families in the area were Harrison, Taylor, Hedgepeth, Harper, and Wheless. (NCDAH.)

The community of Castalia was settled around 1850 and incorporated in 1873. By 1900, it had a population of 168. The town had a Baptist and a Primitive Baptist church, and Mrs. S.J. Barthelomew ran the only hotel. Her husband owned the Barthelomew & Company General Store. Mrs. J.S. Terry had a millinery shop. T.A. Matthews was the town doctor, and W.B. Harper was the dentist. The 1990 population of Castalia was just over 260. (NCDAH.)

Castalia has had a school since 1853. R.D. Richardson founded the school and is credited with naming the community Castalia, from the Castalian Springs at Mt. Parnassus in Greece. In 1880, W.O. Dunn opened the Castalia Academy, which was a boarding school with dorms for both girls and boys. This public school opened in the 1920s as one of several Rosenwald schools in the county. In 1948, the high school closed, and the elementary school closed in 1966, when Nash County began to consolidate schools. (NCDAH.)

In 1895, Dr. H.B. Battle photographed five generations of a family working on the R.H. Ricks farm in Nash County. The oldest couple are Ben and Harriet Speight (on the right) and their great-grandchild Georginna Harrison. The other couples are Jonas and Delia Harrison, George and Gabrella Harrison, and Jeff and Jane Bell. (Barringer.)

These men are "cropping," or "priming," tobacco. Beginning in late June and lasting throughout the summer, field hands, usually men, would pull the lower leaves off the tobacco stalks and drop them in a basket or container pulled by mules down the rows. A field could be cropped at least three times during a season. (NCDAH.)

Tobacco became a major crop in the 1880s and continued to be until the 1960s. Tobacco leaves were pulled from the stalks from the bottom up and taken to a shelter. This white mule is pulling the basket to hold the tobacco these farm hands are pulling in the late 1930s on the Watson farm. When mechanization arrived in the 1950s, the workers would ride on the back of a picker pulled by a tractor to pull the leaves. (NCDAH.)

Baskets are stacked against a shelter, where tobacco would be tied to the sticks, then hung in a barn for curing. (NCDAH.)

Around 1910 on the Meyer Ricks farm, tobacco was gathered in boxes and pulled to the barn. In the lower left of the photograph is a horse/mule-drawn cultivator, which was used to smooth a field after disking. (NCDAH.)

By the 1940s, tractors were used to pull riders who set out the tobacco plants that had been raised in a small bed in the early spring. The mechanism on the tractor poked a hole in the ground so that the men could insert the shoots of tobacco. Then the machine would spray water on the shoot and close the hole around the plant. (Barringer.)

Tobacco taken to the barns was tied to the sticks for drying. This scene is on the Braswell farm near Battleboro in the 1940s. (NCDAH.)

Traditionally, women and older children did the tying, or looping, as it was called in some areas. Men used to work in the fields and lift the baskets of tobacco. Younger children would learn by watching their parents, and they would begin as "handers," which meant handing leaves of tobacco to the loopers, who would tie it to the sticks. Some farms employed children as young as six or seven to hand tobacco to the skilled loopers, working faster than the camera. (NCDAH.)

Once the green tobacco was all tied, the sticks were taken to a barn and cured by heating to high temperatures for several weeks. Often children between the ages of 10 and 13 would be used to hang the tobacco because they were good at climbing up the rafters. Oliver Williams is "putting in" a crop of tobacco around 1950. (Barringer.)

Once the tobacco was cured, it would be removed from the barn and sorted, or "graded," and the leaves of similar quality would be tied together into a bundle. These women are grading tobacco in the 1940s. Grading was a skill that many good workers strove for because the best bundles would bring the best prices at the tobacco warehouses. (NCDAH.)

"Rose Hill" originally was a 9,000-acre plantation in central Nash County in the Corinth community owned by Nathan Boddie, "the Father of Nash County." In 1792, Nathan built this house for his son, George. It was remodeled in the 1870s, but retained the large porch with Doric columns. In 1967, the mansion was given to Wesleyan College, and it is used for meetings and receptions. (NCWC.)

This photograph is of the interior of Rose Hill, which was put on the National Register in 1982. (NCWC.)

As part of the 1965 Nash County Harvest Festival, each Nash County community sent a Miss and a Mrs. Representative. These women are standing on the steps of the Cooley Home in Nashville, home of Congressman Harold D. Cooley, standing in the top right. Brenda Murray (Moore), #7, was Miss Aventon. Her mother, Jane Saunders, was Mrs. Aventon, to the left of #29. Miss Dortches was #14. Eunice Griffin was Mrs. Red Oak, #33, and Miss Red Oak was JoAnn Rose (King), #10. (Saunders.)

Two

BATTLEBORO, WHITAKERS, AND NORTHEAST NASH

Located in northeastern Nash County, Battleboro and Whitakers are in both Nash and Edgecombe County, as the railroad that runs through the center of both towns is the county line. Situated between Battleboro and Whitakers along Interstate 95, Gold Rock is no longer an incorporated town. Gold Rock's many hotels and restaurants serve interstate travelers, which outnumber the local residents.

Started in 1835 as Battle's Camp along the railroad, which was being built by Joseph S. Battle and incorporated in 1873 as Battleboro, the community grew to a population of 229 by 1900. The town had three churches, St. John's Episcopal, First Baptist Church, and the Methodist church. St. John's, which was built in 1891, suffered a terrible fire in 1996, but has been restored. A 1902 fire burned the entire business district, but the citizens rebuilt. By 1990, the population had almost doubled to 447. Rocky Mount annexed the community into its city limits in 1996, and Battleboro no longer is recognized as a town.

Richard and Elizabeth Carey Whitakers settled along Fishing Creek in the mid-1700s and gave their name to the community. Around 1840, the Wilmington-Weldon Railroad built a turnout, known as Whitakers Turnout, which led to the town. The first post office opened in 1869, and the town was incorporated three years later. The population in 1900 was 388. At that time the area had three grocery stores, six general stores, a livery stable, two sawmills, and two cotton gins. By the 1940s, Whitakers also had a theater, a cafe, a barbershop, a tin shop, and a pool room. Consolidated Diesel, between Whitakers and Battleboro, opened in 1983, a combined project of J.I. Case and Cummins Engine Co. to produce diesel engines. Many of the retail stores are gone, yet Whitakers has a medical clinic, a private academy, and several churches to serve the more than 850 residents living there today.

Built in the late 1850s, Bellamy's Mill on Fishing Creek is the only stone mill in Nash County. Listed on the National Register for Historic Places, the three-story mill was a gristmill and served as a factory during the Civil War. A mill had been on this site since 1817 and had gone through various owners including Grant, Whitaker, Branch, and Hunter before Jon T. Bellamy acquired the property and built this structure. (Barringer.)

In 1910, Florence Rux Draughon was photographed with her daughter, Margaret. The Draughons farmed on the Edgecombe side of Whitakers, but they lived on the Nash side of the town, one block west of present-day Highway 301. (O'Brien.)

This is a photograph of Otis Edward's family in Battleboro in the 1920s. Edwards managed the W.E. Edwards & Son Mercantile Store. His father's home was in Red Oak. Other general stores included T.P. Braswell and Son, W.S. Bulluck, and F.M. Rawlings. (Saunders.)

Here is Jarrette White and his wife, Corneila Moore, in 1897. White was the principal of Whitakers School in the early 1900s and later served as the mayor of Whitakers. (O'Brien.)

Pictured here is the Reverend Herman Baum and his wife, Leda Leigh Draughon, and children, Betty and Becky Baum. He was the minister of the Whitakers Methodist Church. His wife, Leda Leigh, helped establish the library in Whitakers and assisted in many community activities. She was instrumental in helping the area grow. (O'Brien.)

Hearne Brothers & Company operated in Whitakers from about 1900 through the 1920s producing caskets. The second man from the right in overalls is Luther Jones around 1920. (Tippett.)

Luther Jones married Maggie Griffin on September 5, 1920, and they moved into this house on Nash Street one block from the railroad tracks on the Nash County side of Whitakers. They raised nine children in this typical family home, which Maggie always had trimmed with flowers. When the house was first built, there was just a dirt track for wagons. In the 1950s, a newly paved highway took most of the front yard. (NCDAH.)

Luther Jones was born in Nash County in 1894, the son of William Frank Jones and Lougenia Bryant Jones. Luther worked at various jobs around Whitakers, including the Hearne casket company, but mostly for the railroad, loading freight at the depot in the center of town. Luther died in 1944, leaving Maggie to raise their nine children and a son from an earlier marriage. This picture of Luther was taken in late 1943. (Tippett.)

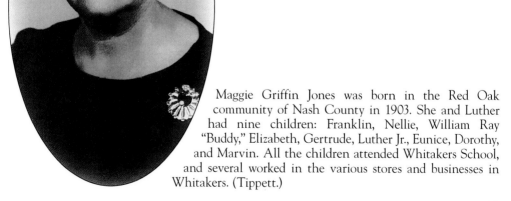

Maggie Griffin Jones was born in the Red Oak community of Nash County in 1903. She and Luther had nine children: Franklin, Nellie, William Ray "Buddy," Elizabeth, Gertrude, Luther Jr., Eunice, Dorothy, and Marvin. All the children attended Whitakers School, and several worked in the various stores and businesses in Whitakers. (Tippett.)

One of the largest farms in the Battleboro area was the Braswell Farm. In the late 1930s or early 1940s, a community meeting was held at the farm. (NCDAH.)

An old Southern tradition, dating back to the 1700s, is a barbecue. Whole hogs are split and cooked over wood coals for most of a day and seasoned with a vinegar-based sauce. Then the diners either picked the meat off the pigs, hence the name pig-picking, or it was chopped into fine meat and served with cole slaw, potatoes, and Brunswick stew. (NCDAH.)

Brunswick stew is traditionally cooked in a large pot over an open fire. The ingredients normally include chicken, tomatoes, potatoes, onions, corn, lima beans, and seasonings. A stew cook often produces dozens of quarts, which can be frozen. Many area schools, churches, and fire departments still have stews as fund-raisers. (NCDAH.)

This may be Thomas Pearsall addressing citizens in northern Nash County at a community meeting on the Braswell Farm in the 1940s. Born in Rocky Mount, Pearsall attended Rocky Mount Senior High School and UNC-Chapel Hill, where he earned a law degree. He was appointed to the North Carolina General Assembly and elected for three more terms. Pearsall was speaker of the house in 1947. Instrumental in the integration plan in North Carolina, Pearsall helped reorganize the UNC system and establish North Carolina Wesleyan College. (NCDAH.)

The railroad first came to Whitakers in 1840. By the 1880s, a depot was in place for passengers and small freight. Although the tracks still divide the town and trains go through on a daily basis, none stop anymore, so the depot was removed. (NCDAH.)

Completed in 1922, Whitakers School served grades 1 through 11. The first school in the area was Whitakers Academy, opened by Andrew J. Moore in 1876. The high school merged with Red Oak in 1963, and the elementary school continued until 1966. The school was closed then, but later purchased by a group to become the home of Enfield Academy, a private school that began in 1970. This building was condemned in 1998 and is scheduled to be demolished and replaced by a modern structure.

Three

AVENTON, HILLIARDSTON, AND RED OAK

CO-AUTHORED BY GRETCHEN JOURNIGAN

Aventon and Hillardston are two of the oldest communities in the county, with a current population under 300 people each. Named after Jim Avent, who settled the area around 1740, the first post office was Aventsville, but eventually changed to Aventon. Five generations of the Avent family operated a country store. In 1840, Aventon Academy opened. Mr. George Ward founded a general store in 1915, which closed in the 1980s.

John Hilliard settled the area around 1780, and Hilliardston became the richest agricultural segment of the county. A stop on the Louisburg to Tarboro and Richmond to Raleigh stage routes, the crossroads also had an academy dating to 1807.

Red Oak has a population of just over 300 and is the largest community in northern Nash County. Settled in the late 1880s, Red Oak acquired its name from the grove of trees there. Incorporated in 1965, it is the youngest town in Nash County. Despite the small population, the community is one of the strongest supporters of school athletic teams. Red Oak had its first high school in 1907. North Carolina's second Farm Life School opened in 1914. Teachers included K.H. McIntyre, Nannie Lee McIntyre, and L.S. Inscoe. Inscoe became the early county historian, and the current Nash-Rocky Mount School System office is named after him.

This aerial photo of Red Oak was probably taken in the 1960s. The Red Oak High School, in the middle with the gym to the left, was the center of community activity, since the turn of the century when an earlier school was there. The original girl's dormitory is the large building on the lower right, which later was a teacherage. The school closed in 1966 with the consolidation of area high schools. (Journigan.)

One of the oldest Baptist churches in the county was organized in 1755 on Fishing Creek in what was then Edgecombe County, which became Halifax County in 1758. In the 1870s, when the old building was torn down, this structure was built across the creek in Nash County as Fishing Creek Baptist Church. In 1948, a new brick church was built to replace this one. (Saunders.)

The first wedding in the new Fishing Creek Church was bride Jackie Saunders and groom George Griffin on July 9, 1950. Others in the wedding party included, from left to right, the following: Billy Griffin, Clare Giddons (the maid of honor), Linda Journigan (flower girl), groomsmen William Gray Saunders and Willis Griffin, and bridesmaids Peggy Saunders Harris and Verna D. Avent. (Faulkner.)

This photograph is of an Aventon School group around 1910 with Gattis Murray sitting on the shoulders of another boy. Aventon was one of over 100 community schools in the early 1900s. (Hicks.)

Here is Mary Arrington Sumner and her great-grandson, Fred Hicks, in 1911. Mrs. Sumner was a descendant of Arthur and Nick Arrington. Nick Arrington was infamous in Nash County for having cockfights in the 1820 and 1830s. (Hicks.)

Pictured here is Mary Alfred Cooper Hicks with her son, Fred, and her daughter, Sarah, in a 1915 motorcycle with a sidecar. Mrs. Hicks inherited one of the oldest homes in Nash County dating to the early 1780s. The Battle-Cooper-Hicks house has been passed down in the same family for 200 years. (Hicks.)

Fred Hicks (motorcycle driver seen above) and Hortense Murray were married in 1946 after Fred returned from army service in Europe. They farmed in the Aventon community. (Hicks.)

Pictured here is Hortense Murray around 1938 by the Journigan store in Aventon. (Hicks.)

Here is Lola Avent with Karen Hicks, daughter of Fred and Hortense Hicks, around 1950. Lola took care of many of the children in the Aventon area. (Hicks.)

Caroline Virginia Barnhill, born in Enfield in nearby Halifax County, married John Robert Ward in October 1911. (Skinner.)

Pictured here is John Robert Ward and Wade Avent around 1910. Both men worked at the sawmill. (Skinner.)

Dorothy Ward was born in July 1912 to Caroline and John Robert Ward, and this photo was taken the next year, illustrating Dorothy's interest in music. (Skinner.)

Dorothy Ward married Sam Skinner in May 1930 and had three children, Jackie, Peggy, and J.L., seen here in 1941. (Skinner.)

John Hilliard inherited a farm from his father around 1800 and built a late Georgian style plantation house called "Black Jack." The house was put on the National Register in 1974, along with a similar house, "The Meadows," built by John's brother, Robert Carter Hilliard. John Hilliard would serve in the North Carolina General Assembly in the early nineteenth century. (NCDAH.)

According to the *Nash County Historical Notes*, Black Jack "is among the earliest and best preserved plantation houses exemplary of the fine traditional craftsmanship characteristic of the area" (p. 309). The two-and-a-half-story structure is a hall and parlor plan with an enclosed stair to the second level. (NCDAH.)

The Hilliardston School, located "above the fall of the rivers," was advertised in the early 1820s in the Raleigh paper. Mr. Stone was the first tutor. In 1825, a female department was added to teach academic subjects "along with Drawing and Painting and Plain and Ornamental Needlework." (NCDAH.)

Philadelphia Academy and Philadelphia Church were located between Hilliardston and Red Oak. Nearby was the Marnes Methodist Church, the oldest African-American church in the county. (NCDAH.)

Nurse Rachel Kellum was not the first registered nurse in Nash County. That honor goes to Mary Cecilia Rose of Washington, who moved to Nash in 1909 and became Mrs. S.T. Anderson. Miss Kellum also relocated to this area and was active as a home nurse in the Red Oak and Rocky Mount area before joining the staff of the Sanitarium Hospital. (Saunders.)

Jack Avent joined the navy, and his brother, Robert, joined the army in WW II. Jack is sitting on the curb of the railroad tracks on Main Street in Rocky Mount in 1943. His son, Elliot, would become the head baseball coach at N.C. State. (Saunders.)

Pictured here is Sterling Journigan in front of his store, which he started in Aventon in the early 1920s. In addition to running the store, Sterling managed a farm. He died in 1980 and had worked in the store for 60 years. His son, Neal, kept the store running while his other sons, Ransom and Richard Journigan, continued to farm. (Journigan.)

Pictured here are Sterling Journigan's three children, Ransome Journigan, Richard Journigan, and Linda Journigan (Faulkner), in front of the old Saunders homeplace in the early 1950s. Ransome and Richard farmed, and their sister married and moved to Red Oak. (Journigan.)

Here is Mrs. Mary Ann Gardner Saunders with a nurse around 1900. Miss Gardner married James Royal Saunders in 1868, and they raised five children. (Saunders.)

Pictured here are Ludie Saunders, James Royal Saunders Jr. (son of Mrs Saunders seen above), and children Mary Louise (Journigan) and Edna Mae (Alvenson) around 1925. (Journigan.)

Here is John A. Saunders on a pony in 1949. He is the eldest son of John M. and Annie Mae Saunders. (Saunders.)

The Red Oak High School Class of 1913 was the last class before the Farm Life School was established the next year. This was the only high school in the northern part of the county. (Fisher.)

The Red Oak High School baseball team won the state championship for the second time in two years in 1921. The members of the team, from left to right, are as follows: (front row) T.B. Faulkner, Henry Lee Griffin, Jack Green, and Bernard Faulkner; (middle row) Centell "Touchdown" Jones, Clarence Beal, and Harry Whitaker; (back row) Coach Conley Stewart, "Legs" Faulkner, Dr. Sam Jones, and Harvey Edwards. (E. Moore.)

Sports were an important activity in the various communities, and each school took pride in their teams and supported them. The 1926–27 Red Oak basketball team were the Nash County champions, indicating that baseball, although popular, was not the only strong sport in the area. (E. Moore.)

The 1944–45 girls basketball team was coached by the new principal, J.A. Martin. (Fisher.)

Pictured here is the 1944 boys basketball team. Coach Bill Ennis took the baseball team to the state championship in both 1945 and 1946. While the basketball team never won a title, they did compete in the state playoffs, finishing second in five different years and finishing third twice during the 1940s. (Fisher.)

Red Oak Baptist Church was established in the 1840s. For a short time, the church was moved and renamed Rehobeth, but it returned to Red Oak in 1884. The Rehobeth church closed in the 1890s. (NCDAH.)

Pictured here, from left to right, are the following: (front row) Molly Beal, William "Ed" Edwards, and Preacher May of the Red Oak Baptist Church; (back row) Lillie and Annie Edwards (daughters of William Edwards), and Alex Whitley. (Saunders.)

This scene is of the Edwards House in Red Oak, which was completed in 1897. Pictured here are W.E. Edwards and his wife, Virginia Whitley Edwards, with baby Lillie and daughter, Mary, to her left. Their sons included Arthur, Jim, Eddie, Bud, Otis, Willie, and Sol. The four men in the back were construction workers completing the house when a traveling photographer stopped by. The house was hit by a tree in 1996 during Hurricane Fran, but has been restored. (Saunders.)

D.H. "Bud" Edwards was just a child when his parents' house was being built on the previous page. He served in WW I and came home to marry a local girl. (Saunders.)

Pictured here is Bud's older brother, Arthur Edwards, and his wife, Mae Whitely Edwards, of Red Oak. Another brother, Otis, married and moved to Battleboro. (Saunders.)

Pearl Ervin married Bud Edwards and taught school at Red Oak for almost 40 years, mostly first grade. (Saunders.)

Jane Edwards (Saunders) is the daughter of Pearl and Bud Edwards. This photograph was taken around 1934. (Saunders.)

Pictured here is Sullivan Fisher (right) winning the Grand Champion ribbon with Blackout at the 4-H Meat Animal Show and Sale in 1943. The show was held at the Eastern Carolina Livestock Arena on Highway 97. Mr. Fisher was known for 50 years as the leading breeder of steers in Nash County. (Fisher.)

Mr. Fisher taught his daughters to appreciate livestock, and they were all active in 4-H activities. Pictured here are Nancy Fisher (Marshall), Linda Fisher, and Betty Anne Fisher with Buffor, 4-H steer in 1976. (Fisher.)

Here is Nancy Fisher (Marshall) with her blue ribbon champion steer in 1980 at the Eastern Carolina Livestock Show with the buyer, J.R. Wordsworth and family. Mr. Wordsworth is the owner of Meadowbrook Meat Co. and J.R.'s Steakhouse in Rocky Mount. (Fisher.)

Anne Journigan won her first 4-H ribbon when she was nine years old. A dozen years later, in 1998, she graduated from N.C. State University with a degree in animal science. (Journigan.)

This is Mr. Theodore Faulkner (left) in his store with Mr. Ronnie Batchelor. Batchelor was the president of the Red Oak branch of Planters Bank. Faulkner's store is a familiar landmark in Red Oak. (E. Moore.)

This scene is the Memorial Day Parade in 1976 with Theodore Faulkner in the back of the wagon with Jan Michael, Bo, Deborah, Leigh, Anne Graves, and Joe Arrington driving. Faulkner's store is in the background. (E. Moore.)

Four

BAILEY, SPRING HOPE, AND SOUTHERN NASH

Southern Nash County is dotted with farms and towns such as Bailey, Momeyer, Spring Hope, Middlesex, and Stanhope, some of which are too small to be incorporated. Bailey was settled just before the Civil War; however, it was not chartered until 1908, when a rail line came to town. The first school in the area was at Rock Spring. Later, the girls basketball team would go for four straight seasons without a loss, creating one of the longest high school winning streaks in the state. The oldest business is Farmer Chevrolet, which opened in 1910. John Momeyer opened a sawmill about the same time at a crossroads called Bass. The lumber company grew and a railroad came to Momeyer to ship the timber. Today, Momeyer has a population of around 270, and Bailey has one of about 570.

West of Bailey is Spring Hope, the third largest town in Nash County. Today, Spring Hope has a population of almost 1,300, but when it was incorporated in 1887, it had a total population of 50 people and three saloons. The railroad was rerouted around Webb's Mill, a station was built at the end of the line, and Spring Hope began. The community had a brickyard, a turpentine distillery, a cotton oil mill, a fertilizer factory, and a wagon factory. By 1910, the population had topped 1,600 and included a thriving community of clothing stores, general stores, saloons, bookstores, and drugstores. The town began a newspaper in the 1930s, and in 1947, Allen Barbee began the weekly *Spring Hope Enterprise,* which recently celebrated its 50th anniversary. Spring Hope hosts the annual Pumpkin Festival each fall.

Webb's Mill dates to the middle of the 1880s. James T. Webb started the building, which bears his name, but he died in 1887 before the mill was finished. Webb's Mill was later owned by L.M Edwards, C.W. Lassiter, Joe Privatte, and George Wheless. The mill was used to grind corn. (NCDAH.)

Established by a state charter in 1967, the Country Doctor Museum has grown from this house to a complex of several buildings that tell the story of medicine in rural areas. This building is two doctors' offices and houses equipment from over a century ago. Behind the doctor's office is a medicinal garden. Other buildings include a nursing museum and the Carriage House, which displays the means doctors used to make house calls, from saddle to buggy to early car. (CDM.)

Dr. Josephine Newell was the force behind this museum. She was one of the first female doctors in southern Nash County and comes from seven generations of family doctors. She helped the complex grow to include a library in the Farmer Annex, where researchers can come and study the journals and materials of doctors from the past century. The museum has apothecary bottles from old drugstores. (CDM.)

Less than 100 years old, Middlesex has a population of about 900. Incorporated in 1908, the community grew up around a railroad line and was named for the English community. Mrs. John J.R. Finch was the first postmistress in 1909. The major business in the area was Dennis-Simmons Lumber Co. Middlesex First Baptist Church was organized in 1908 by Reverend Pippen. This church building was completed in 1938. (NCDAH.)

Middlesex Depot was completed in 1906 along the Norfolk Southern Railway. In 1915, Middlesex incorporated the Free Will Baptist Children's Home, which covered 400 acres and various buildings. Today, Middlesex is home to almost 1,000 residents. (NCDAH.)

Built in 1910, the Spring Hope First Baptist Church serves as a transition between the residential and business districts of the town. The minister then was Reverend D.F. Putnam. Located on the corner of Nash and Walnut Streets, this church is still in operation in this building. (ECUSC.)

The train is passing through the town around 1910. Today, the depot is the town library. Spring Hope has a delightful museum, which houses a large collection of historic photographs. The building in the background is now a dry cleaners. (NCDAH.)

In 1910, Spring Hope had five hotels and boardinghouses. They were managed by Mrs. J.J. Spivey, Nick Collie, George Spivey, James Taborn, and J.J. Sanders. This hotel was located on the corner of Nash and Pine Streets, but is no longer standing. (NCDAH.)

Pictured here is Spring Hope's first car. (NCDAH.)

The Sylvester Brantley–Herring House was built around 1825 and is located in Stanhope, a community named for Earl of Stanhope. The community developed at the crossroads between Richmond and Raleigh to Tarboro roads. Early families included Baines, Brantley, Ricks, Bissett, and Strickland. Dr. Robert H. Wright, the first president of East Carolina Teacher's College, now East Carolina University, was a principal at Stanhope Academy. (NCDAH.)

Taylor's Mill Pond is located in the extreme southern corner of Nash County and borders Wilson County. The mill was one of almost four dozen mills scattered throughout the county to use the power created by the numerous falls along the streams and rivers. (NCDAH.)

Five

ROCKY MOUNT

In a 1950s travel guide, Rocky Mount was known for four things: the home of Kay Kyser, Melton's Barbecue, the June German, and Bugs Barringer. The city, which began as a mill and railroad community, grew to become the leading tobacco market in the world and was also recognized for its culture. Kay Kyser was a popular musician. Bob Melton had established one of the oldest and most successful barbecue restaurants in the East. The June German began in 1880 as a summer dance and became the social event of North Carolina. Bugs Barringer recorded it all with his camera as Rocky Mount continued to grow as the largest city in northeastern North Carolina between Raleigh and the coast.

The first settlers arrived in the 1740s, and by 1816, James C.B. Atkinson served as the first postmaster for the post office, named Rocky Mount, for the rocks at that falls. The oldest church, Falls of the Tar River Primitive Baptist Church, was established in 1757 and is still in operation today, although the original building was replaced in 1927.

A village grew around the mill, and after the railroad arrived, the town stretched from the falls to the depot. In 1867, Benjamin Bunn led the campaign to incorporate Rocky Mount. A century later, Rocky Mount would be home to a fast food chain, an office equipment company, textile and furniture plants, and a pharmaceutical company.

The first professional baseball team in Rocky Mount began in 1909 with the minor-league Railroaders. A young Jim Thorpe played on the team and would later lose his 1912 Olympic medals because he was considered a professional. In 1970, Rocky Mount earned the honor of All American City, and Booker T. Washington High School closed, as the students attended Rocky Mount Senior High School to comply with federal desegregation. Called the "Red Carpet City" in the 1970s, Rocky Mount became "The City on the Rise" in the late 1980s, and today is the "Gateway" to eastern North Carolina.

Rocky Mount began as a small post office at the Falls of the Tar and slowly grew as a mill community until the coming of the railroad. The first train in 1840 spurred the growth of the area, which exploded at the turn of the century when Rocky Mount became a railroad boom town. (NCDAH.)

Joel Battle, Peter Evans, and Henry Donaldson built the mill in 1818 that became Rocky Mount Mills in 1825. Eventually, Battle bought out the others, and a member of the Battle family owned or managed the mill until it closed in 1996. This photograph is of the second mill on the site. The first was burned in a Union raid in July 1863. The mill was rebuilt, but burned again in 1867. Today, only the cotton mill, rebuilt in 1869, remains. (Barringer.)

Benjamin Battle built this house in 1835 that was later used as the mill office. Benjamin and his brother, William, sons of Joel Battle, eventually sold the mill to an Uncle James Battle. The large Federal style home was occupied by a Battle until 1918, when it became the mill office. Nearby, the superintendent's office was built around 1830. There were also several mill houses for employees, built in the later half of the nineteenth century and updated in the 1940s. (Barringer.)

Elisha Battle settled along the Tar River in the 1740s. His grandson, Joel, founded Rocky Mount Mills and his descendents were active in Rocky Mount history. Called the "Father of Rocky Mount" in one newspaper story, Thomas Hall Battle (right) was a grandson of the original builder of the mill. Battle would be the founder of the Bank of Rocky Mount, the first bank in the area. He was also president of the first savings and loan bank. Along with Robert Ricks, William Thorpe, Benjamin Bunn, and others, Battle created the Rocky Mount Chamber of Commerce. He served on the Rocky Mount School Board for 34 years. CEO of Rocky Mount Mills, Battle died in 1936. (Barringer.)

In the early part of the twentieth century, the mill continued to prosper. In 1900, it operated 25,000 spindles. By WW II, that number increased to 43,000 spindles and 18,000 twister spindles. The plant was completely renovated and updated after the war and continued to employ hundreds of local residents until it closed. (Barringer.)

Bennet Bunn built "Stonewall" around 1830, the first brick house in Nash County. The stones shaping the front wall were collected along the Tar River. Bunn was a Nash County planter and businessman in Rocky Mount in the 1830s and 1840s. The house, located just off Falls Road, faces Highway 64. Listed on the National Register of Historic Places, Stonewall is the home of the Nash County Historical Association. (NCDAH.)

Completed in 1844 by Redmund Bunn, "Benvenue" was remodeled in 1889 to this appearance by Benjamin Bunn, the first mayor of Rocky Mount and the second congressman from Nash County. The house became a social center for Rocky Mount, and the first country club in the area developed around it. Today, a school, a community, and a road in Rocky Mount all share the name Benvenue. (NCDAH.)

J.W. Hines built this colonial revival home in 1907. Known as the "ice king," Hines owned and operated several ice plants throughout North Carolina. His home, "MacHaven," is described by Catherine Bisher as "the architectural showplace of the residential area" of west Rocky Mount. (NCDAH.)

Not nearly as fancy as these other homes, this house, constructed around WW I, was important, for it served as the home to the Rocky Mount YWCA until new facilities were built in the 1960s. Finally, the organization moved to Hunter Hill in the 1990s. (Barringer.)

The First Presbyterian Church was a small, but carefully constructed building. It was built in 1879 on land donated by Mr. George Allen of New Bern. Until then, meetings were held upstairs in a cotton gin. In 1909, this building was sold to a black congregation, so a new brick structure was completed. (Barringer.)

W.D. Morton was one of the early pastors of the First Presbyterian Church in its new facilities on Church Street. The congregation would also build several mission churches in the area. (NCDAH.)

Rocky Mount First Baptist Church also began as a small wooden structure, which the congregation outgrew by 1910. This is the 1909 Baraca class with their pastor, Dr. I.M. Mercer. (FBC.)

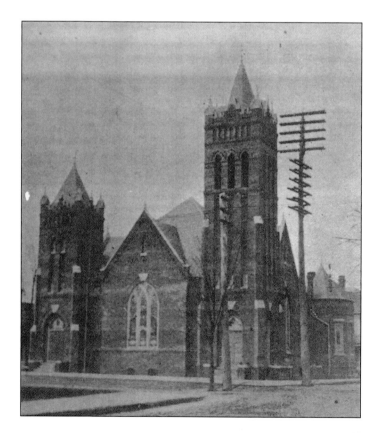

Located on the corner of Sunset Avenue and Church Street, this was the First Methodist Church around 1910, with L.P. Howard and J.B. Thompson as pastors. (Barringer.)

In 1900, the Coghill family posed for this family portrait. Mr. and Mrs. K.W. Coghill (center) are surrounded by the children, their spouses, and a grandson. The children include their son, C. Wesley Coghill, and their daughter, Mrs. H.E. Brewer Sr. (Barringer.)

This c. 1903 photograph is of Mrs. W.A. Warren (right) and her family. (Barringer.)

In 1917, these young ladies posed at Battle Park. From left to right, they are as as follows: (front row) Betsy Henry, Annie Mercer Henry, Elizabeth Whitehead, Lillian Braswell, and Emily Braswell; (back row) Mary McDearman, Sarah Wilkinson, Florence Matthews, Virginia Thorpe, and Tenney Huffines. (Barringer.)

Miss Betty Slade's kindergarten celebrated May Day with a pageant around 1920. (Barringer.)

The Atlantic Coast Line Passenger Depot was completed in 1903 and today is one of the last in eastern North Carolina. The red brick building on the south side of Main Street is Romanesque Revival style and is still used for Amtrak passengers on the north-south run from Florida to Washington, D.C. Just to the right was the Ricks Hotel, the largest in the area at the turn of the century. (BML.)

The Emerson Shops opened in the early 1900s after Atlantic Coast Line selected Rocky Mount to be the hub for its repair shops and engines. During the first half of the twentieth century, Rocky Mount was known as a railroad town, bringing thousands of employees into town. (Barringer.)

The Atlantic Coast Line built its own hospitals for employees around 1905. This building would burn in the 1920s and would be replaced by a brick structure. (ECUSC.)

The railroad also built this magnificent facility in cooperation with the YMCA in 1912 at a cost of $30,000. The basement featured bowling alleys, and the main floor had a reading room and an auditorium. Sleeping quarters were located on the second floor. (BML.)

The streets were not yet paved, but Rocky Mount was obviously growing by 1910. This view down Church Street shows homes and the recently completed Methodist church. (ECUSC.)

Joyner & Rowland, on the corner of Hill and Main Streets, sold hardware, furniture, and appliances. It was the largest retail store in Rocky Mount around 1910. The company also was a cotton brokerage. (Barringer.)

Avents Livestock operated in downtown Rocky Mount. The firm sold horses, saddles, buggies, and harnesses. (Barringer.)

Running east and west, Tarboro Street intersected Main Street and became the focus of business and trade at the turn of the century. (ECUSC.)

Nannie Parker opened her grocery store in 1909 along Raleigh Road. Other early African-American business communities include the Douglas Block, Little Raleigh, and Happy Hill on Thomas, Pine, and nearby streets. (Barringer.)

The Rocky Mount Hosiery Company opened in 1904 with over 200 machines and employed over 200 people The company produced 800 pairs of hoses a day. Mr. J.C. Braswell was president of the company. (NCDAH.)

Richard D. Long operated this saloon on Tarboro Street until Prohibition forced all saloons to close. In 1912, Rocky Mount had over a dozen saloons. One source indicated that this one also served as police headquarters until a station was built for the Rocky Mount Police force. (Barringer.)

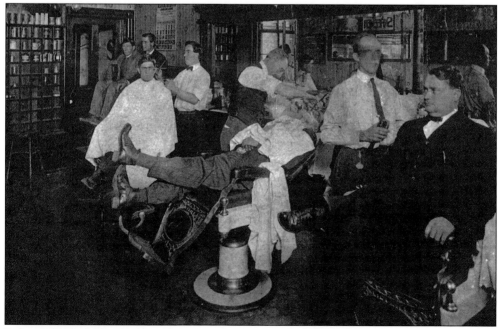

Before WW I, Bobbit's Barber Shop was where the men met to discuss the news and sports. The man in the suit on the right is Walter R. Fountain. (Barringer.)

Rocky Mount Grade School, built in 1901, was the first public school in the area under the program of Governor Charles Aycock. This school would be known as Old West when a complementary Old East would open in 1908. This building was condemned and demolished in 1939, and the new school built in its place was named to honor a school board member and businessman, James C. Braswell. (NRMS.)

Miss Martha "Mattie" Darden is on the steps of Old West with her third grade class around 1910. Her students were Dick Thorp, Alex Thorp, Claude Aycock, Billy Brewer, Ellen Wilkinson, Mary McDearmon, Sara Wilkinson, Florence Matthews, Virginia Throp, Tony Huffins, Betsy Henry, Anna Henry, Elizabeth Whitehead, Lillian Braswell, and Emily Braswell. (Barringer.)

72

Baseball was a popular pastime for both high school and professional teams. The members of the 1910 Rocky Mount Senior High team, from left to right, are as follows: manager Foguetty, Vernon Kyser, Noman Hart, Carlton Gardner, Marvin Murrill, Marvin Hillard, Frank Spruill, Bernard Kinlaw, Rob Arrington, Joe Baker, and Ray "Ducky" Clark. (Barringer.)

The 1914 Rocky Mount High baseball team were the Eastern Division champions in North Carolina. The team members, from left to right, are as follows: (front row) Turner Battle, Bernard Kinlaw, Ryland Harris, Billy Vaughn, and Marvin Robbins; (back row) Coach Mac Wilson, Charlie Harris, Raisley Nunn, Wyche Walker, Hassel Weeks, and Robert Perkinson. (NRMS.)

Baseball was the most popular sport, with semi-professional teams playing in Rocky Mount in 1908, but by 1912, the high school had a basketball team and a football team. (Barringer.)

Built in 1904, the Masonic Temple was located on Main Street. The second floor featured an opera house for touring companies. (ECUSC.)

Founded by Richard H. Ricks, the Ricks Hotel was the finest hotel in eastern North Carolina. Located on Main Street one block from the train depot, the Ricks had its own barbershop and expanded in the 1920s. Although Rocky Mount had three other hotels, including the Cambridge and the Woodard, neither matched the reputation of the Ricks. The hotel was demolished in the 1970s. (Barringer.)

The hotel dining room was a popular place during the breaks of the traditional June German. It was also popular for serving hotel guests and local citizens for Sunday lunch or special occasions. (BML.)

The Rocky Mount Sanitarium opened in 1913 with Dr. L.W. Kornegay and associates. Designed by local architect John C. Stout, the hospital would serve a population of over 10,000. The Sanitarium had approximately 70 beds in the 1950s and admitted both blacks and whites. There would also be a small 30-bed hospital in Nashville by 1955. (NGH.)

Two years after the Sanitarium opened, Parkview Hospital opened and began a nursing school. The hospital was founded by Billy Johnson, and the first doctors included Dr. Whitehead, Dr. R.H. Speight, Dr. I.P. Battle, and chief surgeon Edmund S. Boice. By 1955, Parkview had expanded to over 110 beds with 30 reserved for blacks. This hospital was closed in 1971 when Nash General opened. (NGH.)

With WW I in 1917 came a need for trained nurses. The Red Cross chapter in Rocky Mount saw more service dealing with the influenza epidemic of 1918 than with war casualties. The women set up an additional hospital at the Methodist church. Several of the women died from the flu, contracted while caring for patients or taking food and medicine to them. (Barringer.)

Members of the Red Cross Knitting Club made sweaters and socks for soldiers. Some of the members have been identified as Margaret Davis, Mary Battle, Delfa McCall, Annie Scorsby, Katherine Woodard, and Alice Suiter. (Barringer.)

Edward Epstein came to Rocky Mount in 1905 and opened a men's clothing store in the Masonic Temple building. In 1912, he moved Epstein's Gents Furnishing Store to the corner of Main and Tarboro Streets. (Barringer.)

Epstein's was the clothing store for men for over 75 years, selling everything from hats and suits to overalls. Later, the store expanded to include women's fine clothing. (NCDAH.)

Rosenbloom-Levy began on Main Street in Tarboro in 1910 as a family-owned store offering clothing and accessories. In 1917, they opened this branch on Main Street in Rocky Mount with J.A. Rosenbloom as manager. This is the second-floor sales force with Minnie Rosenbloom seated on the left. Others are Effie Kohler, Louise Horne, Anna Groom, May Teague, Annie Blythe, and Nealie Thomas. In 1972, the company opened a branch in Tarrytown Mall, and in 1976, it opened a men's specialty store, E.S. Levy, on Main Street in Rocky Mount. (Barringer.)

Daniel's Store was located on Tarboro Street before it moved to Main Street in the 1930s. The firm opened in 1905 as a dry goods store under the name, Draper & Daniel Store. By 1910, it was specializing in men's clothing. Next door is Conyer's, another clothing store. (Barringer.)

Little Theatre Guild was organized by Proctor Arrington (top right) in 1920. Members included, from left to right, the following: (front row) Elizabeth Bulluck, Rachel Marshbourn, Nancy Gordon, Joe Green, Mary Meeks, Chloris Tuttle, and Bessie Daughtridge; (middle row) James Bobbitt, Hatcher Kinchelow, Lindsay Dail, H.S. Pool Jr., Graham Dozier, and Charles Ivey; (back row) T.E. Wagg, Henry Ricks, Delmont Griffin, and A.L. Borden. Miss Bulluck, in the front row, was the daughter of the founder of Bulluck's Department Store. Shortly after this photo, she married Hatcher Kinchelow, who would later manage the store. (Bulluck's.)

Through the efforts of the Rocky Mount Women's Club and the fine contributions of Dr. Mark Russell Braswell, the Thomas Hackney Braswell Memorial Library was created and has served Rocky Mount for over 75 years. During WW I, the library collection was moved to the chamber of commerce office and opened to the public in 1921. When Dr. Braswell's son, Thomas, died at the age of 12, Dr. Braswell provided the funds for a new library building, which opened in 1923. (NCDAH.)

Tobacco became a major commercial crop in northeastern North Carolina in the 1880s. The first warehouse in Nash County was in Battleboro in 1885 by T.P. Braswell. By 1887, Rocky Mount Warehouse had opened, followed in 1889 by the Nash Warehouse. By 1895, there were four warehouses in Rocky Mount, and they were selling over 7 million pounds of tobacco. Thorpe and Ricks opened a facility to process tobacco, the only such facility in eastern North Carolina. Rocky Mount became the center for tobacco trade. (NCDAH.)

The National Bank of Rocky Mount was built on the corner of Tarboro and Main Streets. It was completed in 1918 with a two-story base and four more stories rising above the downtown, making it one of Rocky Mount's first skyscrapers. (Barringer.)

By 1915, the Rocky Mount Police Department had a paddy wagon, one bicycle, and a dog. Members of the force included Bud Harris, Oliver Wheeless, A.A. Parrish, Sid Taylor, Eli Stephenson, Jimmie Reams, George Denny, Sid Davis, W.L. Thorp, Henry Hedgepeth, and Police Chief Oliver Hedgepeth. (Barringer.)

By 1934, the police department had expanded. From left to right, as listed on the back of the photograph, are the following: (front row) Officers W.C. Walston and Lou Sumner; (second row) Chief Bill Bailey, O.P. Hedgepeth, E.L. Stephenson, Sid Taylor, and Boo King; (third row) Z.H. Wheeless, G.L. Pittman, G.N. William, A.F. Powell, J.B. Robinson, R. Rogers, M.N. Hinton, and H.N. Hedgepeth; (fourth row) P.C. Zimmerman, C.S. Henry, George Wheeless, and E.W. Gupton. (Barringer.)

Through the Works Project Administration, formed because of the Great Depression in the 1930s, Rocky Mount acquired a new municipal building in 1936 to house the Town's offices and police department. (BML.)

Taylor's Department Store on Main Street in Rocky Mount was one of many clothing establishments. In front of the store is the Rocky Mount Dog Catcher Truck. (Barringer.)

According to the 1902 city directory, W.T. Rose operated a blacksmith shop in Rocky Mount. By 1906, he was also operating a carriage shop. Six years later, the company was listed as Rose & Son, when Howard Rose joined the firm located on Washington and Tarboro Streets. In 1920, the firm became one of the first Buick dealerships in North Carolina. (Barringer.)

These women appear as if they are about to take a drive in this new car in 1928, although women couldn't legally drive in North Carolina until the 1930s. (Barringer.)

Davenport Motors sold Pontiacs in the 1930s. The car dealership would change locations several times and change dealerships, as well. Today, the company is located off Winstead Avenue and is a Honda and Dodge dealer. (Barringer.)

Another car dealership was Hoggard-Vann Motors, which sold Oldsmobiles and Hudsons in 1947. (Barringer.)

This view of Main Street and downtown Rocky Mount in the late 1930s was probably taken from the top of the National Bank building. Businesses included Rose's Drugstore, Economy Auto Supply, Citizens Building and Loan, Carolina Electric Company, Montgomery Ward, Quinn's Furniture, and at the far end, the Cameo Theater. In the background are several tobacco warehouses. (BML.)

The Belk family began a clothing store in the 1880s in central North Carolina. By the 1920s, the company had numerous partners in various cities in the Carolinas and Virginia. The different stores included Hudson Belk, Belk Leggett, and in eastern North Carolina, 15 Belk-Tyler stores. This was the first Belk's on Main Street in Rocky Mount in the 1930s. Sometime in the 1940s, it moved into a new building on the corner of Main and Nash Streets. In the 1980s, Belk's, like many stores, vacated downtown to move to Golden East Mall. (Barringer.)

Tarboro Street continued to be a major retail district. Baldwin's Department Store would move in the 1970s to Tarrytown Mall, the first mall in eastern North Carolina. Planters Bank is on the corner opposite the National Bank. Other stores included Bobbit's Auto store, Purvis Dry Cleaners, Citizens Savings and Loan, and Powell Business Equipment Co. (BML-Killibrew.)

Originally on the Edgecombe side of Rocky Mount, the post office moved to Tarboro Street in the 1920s. In 1970, the post office opened a million-dollar facility on Raleigh Road, and the old building was the temporary home of Edgecombe Community College. (BML-Killibrew.)

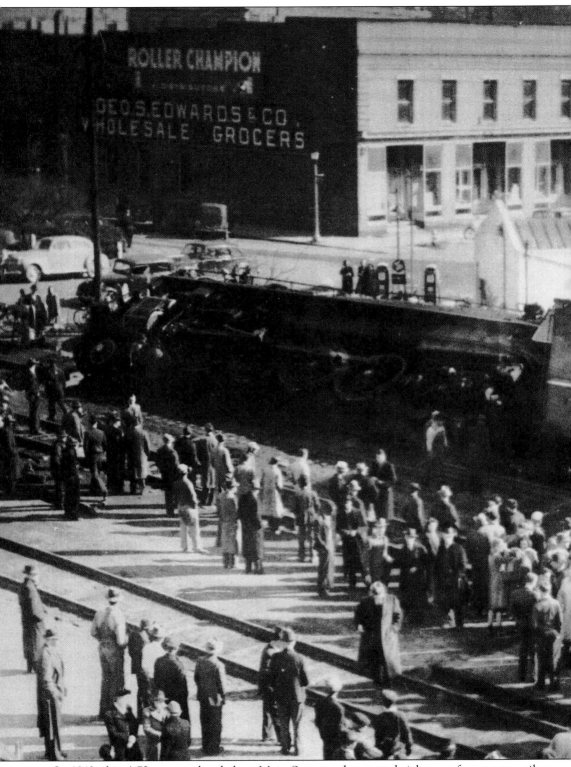

In 1942, this ACL engine derailed on Main Street and attracted sightseers from many miles

around. (Barringer.)

The Rocky Mount Fair has been hosting contests and rides every fall at the fairgrounds since the 1930s. Here, two women prepare the exhibit of award-winning canned goods. Women in the 1930s and 1940s took pride in producing pickles, okra, cucumbers, beets, beans, and many other vegetables for their families. (NCDAH.)

Vernon Sechriest (seen here) was a reporter for the *Rocky Mount Telegram* and active with the Boy Scouts in Nash County. After WW II, Sechriest became the editor of the paper. Josh L. Horne began the *Rocky Mount Telegram* in October 1910, then called the *Morning Telegram*. Although there was already a paper in Rocky Mount, the *Daily Record*, Horne soon bought them out and changed the name of his paper to the *Evening Telegram and Record* in 1912. The paper joined the Associated Press. The offices have recently moved to Tiffany Square. (Hicks.)

Effie Vines Gordon was the Nash County Home Extension agent for many years. She began in 1917 in Edgecombe County and moved to Rocky Mount in 1922. She retired in 1950. (Barringer.)

Rocky Mount schools provided driver education training for both the black and white high schools in the 1950s. (NRMS.)

Many families relocated to Rocky Mount to work for the railroad. John J. Lee and his wife, Annie Edwards Lee, came from Virginia around 1920 and moved into a house on Pender Street. By 1942, when this photo was taken, they had ten children. They were, from left to right, as follows: John Lee (1893–1971); his son John T. (in uniform), who was killed in World War II; Annie (1891–1980); Talmadge "Buddy," who would work for the railroad; Katherine Lee (Martin); Peggy Lee (Every); Clayton Lee; Elsie Lee (Hurst); Eva Lee (Bulluck), who would become a nurse; Doris Lee (Batchelor) and Clyde Lee, who would both work in the mills; and Marie Lee (Perry). (Crowe.)

One of the largest churches in Rocky Mount, First Baptist Church had a Sunday school of over 800 members in 1945. This is the men's class. (FBC.)

First Baptist Church outgrew its small building from the 1880s, and between 1911 and 1912, this new, impressive sanctuary was built on Church Street. Peggy Lee, on the opposite page, will get married here in 1952, one of thousands of marriages in the history of this church. In 1996, First Baptist dedicated a new sanctuary on the opposite side of this block. (FBC.)

Rocky Mount's fourth hospital was Memorial Hospital on the Edgecombe County side of town. It opened in the 1940s. (NGH.)

Another WPA project was the construction of a power plant and city lake in 1935. The lake will become the major park in Rocky Mount. It was dug with shovels and small equipment by local men.

During WW II, the power plant was surrounded by barbed wire fence to protect the facility. In the 1980s, the old plant, which overlooks the Tar River, was remodeled into shops and restaurants. (C. Moore.)

These women are enjoying the June German, a Rocky Mount tradition that began in 1880 near Nobles Mill Pond. The German was always held on a Friday in June, and area African-Americans would have their formal dance the following Monday, using the same decorations. Usually, two orchestras performed at the black-tie affair, including Ozzie Nelson, Jimmy Dorsey, and Rocky Mount's own Kay Kyser. The dances finally ended in 1975; however, recent attempts have been made to revive them. (Barringer.)

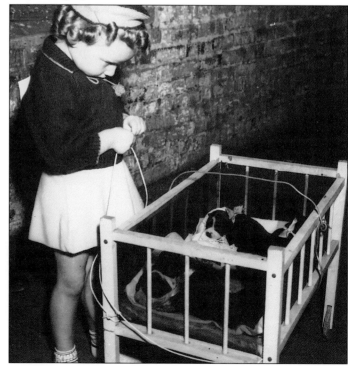

Beginning in the 1930s, as a build-up to the traditional German, a parade, known as the Gallopade, was used to kick off the summer season. It involved the entire community. Here, a young participant makes some preparations before she enters the parade. Gallopade included parades, a horse show and races, an athletic field day, and square dancing. The Gallopade would draw thousands to Rocky Mount during the 1930s. (NCDAH.)

Located on Thomas Street, the Booker T. Theater was completed around 1926 and was originally known as the Savoy. By 1936, the name had been changed to Booker T., and until the 1970s, it was a popular theater for the African-American community in Rocky Mount. During the thirties and forties, movies were shown here for African Americans. (BML.)

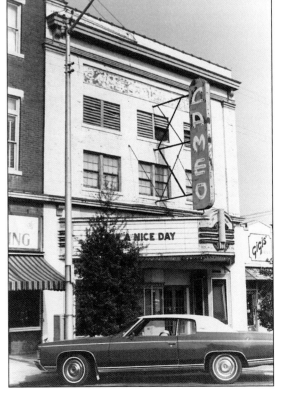

The Cameo Theater was on Main Street about two blocks from the Booker T. Along with the Gem and the Manhattan, the Cameo showed featured Hollywood films. As theaters moved out to the suburbs and to small malls, the downtown theaters all closed. (Barringer.)

A highlight of the 1947 movie season was a visit by Jimmy Stewart and Jane Wyman to promote the movie *Magic Town*, which was about life in small-town America. (Barringer.)

While adults went to the movies, children were taken to the wonderful Children's Museum, located in Sunset Park. Completed in 1952, the museum, the first of its kind in North Carolina, has been educating and entertaining children for almost half a century. The museum's attractions include science exhibits, summer workshops, live animals, and a planetarium.

When Parkview Hospital opened in 1914, there was a strong need for nurses. The next year, the hospital began a nursing school. The doctors taught classes at night, and the nursing students had duty in the hospital in 12-hour shifts. Some were assigned to work in the community. The 1917 class numbered over a dozen, but the 1918 class had only three students because of the war. Over the years, the school grew. This is the 1947 class. By the time Parkview closed in 1971, nurses' training was taking place in area technical/community colleges. (Barringer.)

This photograph is of the 1958 capping exercise for Parkview nurses. They are, from left to right, as follows: (front row) unidentified, Nancy King, Pat Creech, Pat Arrington, Betty Moore, unidentified, Gussie Robinson, Carolyn Bunn, Mavis Mercer, Joan Braswell, Edna Roper, Geraldine Morris, Francis Peedin, Hazel Mercer, unidentified, and Ennis Lucas; (back row) unidentified, Barbara Carter, Barbara Mall, Connie Merritt, Ann Dail, Betty Crisp, Dorothy Neathery, Frances Wood, and Joy Ashby (Gorham).

Pictured here is the Rocky Mount Fire Department in the 1950s. The firefighters, from left to right, are as follows: Peter Mames, Eddie Harper, Troy Brown, Steve Gupton, Van Neal, Perry Ellen, David Shitely, Buck Drummond, Jon Buchan, Tom Daniels, Elwood Inscoe, William Rose, and Herbert Collins. (BML.)

Pictured here is the Rocky Mount Police Department in the 1950s. (BML.)

Uncle Bob, or Colonel Bob Melton, founded one of the most famous barbecue restaurants in North Carolina. Stories have appeared in *Esquire, Town & County,* and *Southern Living,* as well as in newspapers as far away as Sydney, Australia. Born in 1872 in the Castalia community, Robert Benjamin Melton began cooking pigs as a youngster. After trying several professions, he began his little food stand by the river. "Tarheel of the Week" in 1954, he died four years later and was mourned across the state. (Melton.)

In 1924, Bob Melton began selling his seasoned barbecue on the banks of the Tar River. The restaurant grew in popularity as the working class and business people came from all around to sample the traditional recipe, which is still being served. Melton served barbecue, slaw, potatoes, Brunswick stew, and hush puppies, a form of fried corn bread. Later, fried chicken was added. (Melton.)

Because Melton's was so close to the river, it did occasionally flood and have to close down for a day or two to mop out any water. The high-water mark came in September 1996, one week after Hurricane Fran. The floodwaters moved down the river and covered most of the outside of the building, measuring 26 feet above the river. This time the restaurant closed for over a month and spent approximately six more months remodeling the various dining rooms with new floors, paneling, and furniture. These photos are from the second worst flood after Fran, that happened in March 1998. This flood destroyed the photos showing the damage after Fran. (Melton.)

The most famous athlete from Rocky Mount, and definitely the most popular, was Buck Leonard. He was a baseball Hall of Famer who played for the Homestead Grays from 1933 to 1950. He was often called the Black Lou Gherig. Rocky Mount named a little league park after him on Grace Street. Leonard spent his retirement talking to youth groups and neighborhood children about his experiences in the major leagues, while teaching them about sportsmanship. Rocky Mount and the state of North Carolina mourned his loss in November 1997. (Barringer.)

In the 1930s and 1940s, Rocky Mount hosted the Rocks, a Class D Coastal Plain team. In 1942, the Rocks were part of the Bi-State League, but the team was known in 1941 as the Leafs. Team members included George Biershenk at shortstop, Harry Soufas at centerfield, Charley Munday at catcher, Dave Baxter at first base, and Ed Williams as the pitcher. The multi-talented Quentin Martin hit 26 home runs that season, while playing six different field positions, including rightfield and shortstop. George Ferrell managed the team. (NCDAH.)

An unusual feature of Rocky Mount sporting events was this deaf umpire, seen here demonstrating calls to two Rocky Mount Senior High players. (NCDAH.)

Uncle Sam was really a postal clerk named A.C. Davis. He marched in presidential inaugural parades and was always found at local parades, holiday celebrations such as the Fourth of July, and the bicentennial festivities. (NCDAH.)

Scouting was very popular in the 1950s. This is a Rocky Mount troop in 1955. (BML.)

Younger girls spent one or two years as Brownies before being promoted to Junior Girl Scouts. Brownies taught girls teamwork and focused on fun activities, such as roasting marshmallows and making crafts. (BML.)

Children of all ages enjoyed rides on the train at Sunset Park near the Children's Museum. (BML-Killibrew.)

Completed in the 1930s as a small recreational lake, City Lake allowed city kids a chance to enjoy fishing, something county kids, living near the many creeks and rivers, took for granted. In the early 1990s, City Lake, located next to the power plant, was redesigned and features a center fountain, an island for ducks, and decks for fishing. (BML-Killibrew.)

Teenagers liked to visit the teen club in the basement of the Masonic Temple on Main Street. Sibil Haskins, Lyman Melvin, Jimmy Gardner, Nancy Yelverton, Gene Lyons, and Jean Davenport enjoy bottles of Royal Crown Cola, a popular competitor of Pepsi and Coca-Cola in the 1950s. Other popular teen hangouts were the Dairy Bar and the Cake Box on Raleigh Road. (Barringer.)

Younger children were entertained by a puppet show, sponsored by the Rocky Mount Junior Guild in 1958. Eventually, the children would get a real theater for plays and puppet shows. (RMAC.)

Someone in the high school Class of 1961 left a mark on the old water tank on Nashville Road. The City purchased the facility later that year and completely remodeled it. The water tank would be turned into an art gallery on the main floor with a small theater on the second floor. (RMAC.)

The Rocky Mount Arts and Crafts Center opened in the remodeled tank and pumping station in 1963. Each Mother's Day, a large outdoor show and sale features local and regional talent. (RMAC.)

The North Carolina Annual Conference of the United Methodist Church selected Rocky Mount as the location for a new four-year college in 1956. The following year the Rocky Mount Area Wesleyan Foundation began raising money and making plans for the college, which opened September 1959. (NCWC.)

Dr. Thomas Collins (left) was selected as the first president of the college, and he served until 1975. Dr. Bruce Petteway succeeded Dr. Collins in 1975. John A. Vann Jr. (right) was director of the Wesleyan College Foundation in 1966. Vann operated the Oldsmobile dealership in Rocky Mount, formerly known as Hoggard-Vann. (NCWC.)

Although Wesleyan experienced financial difficulties in 1975, the community rallied to support the small private liberal arts college. Today, Wesleyan offers masters programs through an agreement with Campbell University. Recently, Wesleyan opened the Dunn Center, a performing arts center that is the showplace of Nash County. (NCWC.)

The first radio station in Nash County was WEED, which began broadcasting in 1933. In the 1960s, Wesleyan College had its own radio station, WCEC. Dean of Students Sim Wilde (left) is being interviewed by Joe Warner (right). In the 1990s, Rocky Mount would host WRQM, a local public radio station. (NCWC.)

In 1961, Rocky Mount businessmen James Gardner and Leonard Rawls opened a hamburger stand on North Church Street, not far from Braswell Library. It was named for Wilbur Hardee, who began to charcoal grill burgers the year before in Greenville. This was the first of what would become a national chain of fast-food restaurants. (NCDAH.)

Hardee's Headquarters was built in the late 1960s on Church Street, across the Tar River, near what was the municipal airport. Remodeled in the 1980s, this became the national headquarters for the chain, which sold hamburgers, fries, and soft drinks. For many years, Hardee's was one of the largest employers in Rocky Mount. In 1997, the company was purchased by Carl's, a western fast-food chain. (Barringer.)

Two of the popular eating establishments in downtown Rocky Mount were privately owned restaurants, both located on Church Street. Central Cafe, located on the corner of Western and Church Streets across from First Baptist Church, fed most of the employees and customers in downtown Rocky Mount for more than 40 years. The City Lunch, shown here, was known for the best hot dogs in town. It closed around 1990. (BML.)

Planters National Bank is the oldest bank in Rocky Mount, opening in 1899 with James C. Braswell as president. The bank had 31 offices throughout eastern North Carolina by the 1970s. These new headquarters are located on Church Street. (BML.)

Serving residents of Rocky Mount, Edgecombe, and Nash County, the Rocky Mount Edgecombe Community Development Corporation (RMECDC) formed in 1988 to revitalize communities. Directed by Joyce Dickens, the agency works with government agencies, area businesses, and community service providers to create homes and businesses in a revitalized part of Rocky Mount. Projects include Heritage Park, a housing subdivision; Bassett School, renovated into a housing complex; and Enterprise Community, to provide revolving loans and small business assistance. (RMECDC.)

One of the most visible projects of RMECDC is the South Washington Street Revitalization Project at Harambee Square. The photos on this page show the before and after stages. Today, Harambee Square houses the agency's administrative offices, a housing counseling center, a business development center, legal services, job training, Habitat for Humanity, apartments, and several commercial tenants. This is also the location for the annual Harambee Festival, the first weekend in May, which celebrates cultural heritage. (RMECDC.)

Nash General was completed in May 1971, becoming the fifth hospital in Rocky Mount. The medical complex includes the Nash Day Hospital, the Medical Arts Center, and a Health Education Center. When this hospital opened, two of the earlier hospitals, Parkview and Memorial, closed and sent their patients to the new 300-bed facility. RM Day Hospital opened in 1985. (NGH.)

This scene is of the Nash General ribbon cutting in 1971. From left to right are the following: Kemp Battle, who led the campaign for the hospital; Dr. I. Taylor; Mrs. Herman Merrell; Dr. K.D. Weeks, president of the medical staff; and W.S. Williams Jr. Today, the hospital has a staff of over 100 physicians, 1,700 employees, and 400 volunteers. (NGH.)

John Chambliss was born in Rocky Mount in 1921, and he dedicated his life to making life better for those in his hometown. After graduating from the University of North Carolina as an M.D. in 1943, Chambliss earned additional medical training at Harvard. He was a professor of medicine at U.N.C. and vice-president of the medical staff. He was later director of medical education at Nash General. He retired in 1990. Before his death in 1997, Chambliss and his wife, Helen, endowed a professorship of medicine at U.N.C. (NGH.)

This worn doctor's bag belonged to Dr. Chambliss, but it represents the hundreds of doctors who comforted their patients' families while saving lives and giving hope. In 1990, Dr. Chambliss received the Distinguished Internist Award from the North Carolina Chapter of the American College of Physicians. There have been many doctors, and photos of all were not available, but a few to remember are Dr. J.P. Whitehead, I.P Battle, Edmund S. Boice, and Dr. James Grant, the pediatrician who delivered most of Rocky Mount's babies since the 1960s on. (NGH.)

Dr. Newsome Battle was chief surgeon at Parkview Hospital. Born in 1896 in Tarboro, Dr. Battle is a descendant of the family of early settlers of Nash and Edgecombe Counties. After graduating from the University of North Carolina, Dr. Battle began practicing medicine at Parkview. He fell in love with an intern, Margaret White from Michigan, and married her in 1934. They had two children. Dr. Battle was instrumental in getting Nash General Hospital built. He died in 1981. (NGH.)

Dr. Margaret White Battle came to Rocky Mount from the University of Michigan in 1933 to intern at Parkview Hospital. She was the first woman ob/gyn doctor in the county. She met her husband, Dr. Newsome Battle, at Parkview. She retired from medicine in the 1970s after helping establish Nash General Hospital. She spends her free time working for the Nash County Historical Association, which she helped found. She is also completing a 20-year-old project of locating and identifying all the family graveyards in Nash County. (NGH.)

In 1963, the Nash County Board of Education voted to make Benvenue School an Industrial Education Center. Three years later, it became part of the North Carolina Community College system as Nash County Industrial Vocational Center. Jack Ballard was the first president, and he led the development of what became Nash Community Institute in 1969, located at Stoney Creek. In the 1970s, the school moved outside of Rocky Mount to its present location, and in 1987, the facility was renamed Nash Community College. (NCC.)

In 1992–93, a new playhouse opened beside the Tank with a 300-seat auditorium that is used for community events when plays are not being performed. The playhouse has an orchestra pit and a large stage, making it one of the finest community theatres in the state. (RMAC.)

Six

NASH COUNTY PEOPLE

Nash County has been the home of half a dozen congressmen, state politicians, business leaders, athletes, and authors. Talented authors include historians and novelists. In 1938, Julia Cherry Spruill completed *Women's Life and Work in the Southern Colonies*, a classic work still used today in classrooms. Born in Rocky Mount in 1899, Julia taught school there in the 1920s until she married Rhodes scholar Corydon Spruill and moved to Chapel Hill. She earned a master's degree and produced her detailed study on Southern women. She died in 1986, and a prestigious award in women's history is given annually in her honor. Pete Daniel from Spring Hope attended Wake Forest before earning his Ph.D from the University of Maryland. Pete has written half a dozen books on agricultural and Southern history and is currently curator at the Smithsonian Museum of American History. Other historians include Joseph and Helen Watson, who did research on Nash County history, and their son, Alan Watson, a professor at U.N.C.-Wilmington who has also published historical works.

Kaye Gibbons grew up in Nash County and graduated from Rocky Mount Senior High. Her first novel, *Ellen Foster*, became a Hallmark Hall of Fame Special in January 1998 after being a best-seller. Kaye's other novels include *A Virtuous Woman*, *A Cure for Dreams*, and *Charms for an Easy Life*. Allan Gurganus's novel *Oldest Confederate Widow Tells All* also became a best-seller and was a television mini-series. Gurganus received the Sir Walter Raleigh Award and the *L.A. Times* Book Prize.

An earlier writer, Jack Kerouac was not native to Nash, but he spent time visiting his sister's family in Little Easonburg while he worked on his manuscripts. It would be years before the locals realized that Kerouac, the founder of the "Beat movement" in American literature, wrote his classic, *On the Road*, down the road in a Nash County community.

Pictured here is the 1941 school board. The members, from left to right, are as follows: (front row) Mrs. A.P. Thorpe Sr., Mrs. W.H. Horne, J.C. Braswell (chair), R.M. Wilson, and Mrs. Elizabeth Pate (secretary); (back row) John J. Wells, Ben E. Fountain, Kemp D. Battle, L.L. Leavly, C.S. Taylor, and George R. Edwards. Two Rocky Mount schools are named after board members, Braswell and Edwards. (NRMS.)

The Board of Trustees for the Rocky Mount school system in 1920 included many prominent business leaders of the community. They are as follows: 1. Thomas Battle was president, then manager of Rocky Mount Mills; 2. Richard T. Fountain was a judge, a member of the North Carolina General Assembly, and lieutenant governor; 3. Ed Gorham; 4. Maurice V. Barnhill became North Carolina Supreme Court Justice; 5. Lucius V. Bassett served in the North Carolina Senate; 6. John C. Braswell was president of Planters Bank; 7. J.Q. Robinson; 8. Theophilus T. Thorne served as mayor of Battleboro in 1890; 9. W.S. Wilkinson founded the Wilkinson Bulluck Insurance Company and was superintendent of Nash County Schools. (Barringer.)

A Civil War veteran and hero of the Bethel Regiment, Robert H. Ricks was born in Nash County in 1836. After the war, he became president of Rocky Mount Mills, vice-president of the Bank of Rocky Mount, and president of the Rocky Mount Ice Company and the Enfield Hosiery Co. He was also co-founder of Thorpe and Ricks Tobacco Co. (Barringer.)

Pictured here in 1885 is Alex P. Thorpe, one of the founders of Thorpe & Ricks Tobacco Co. (Barringer.)

The first congressman from Nash County was Archibald Hunter Arrington. "Baldy," as Archibald was known, was elected to Congress in 1840 and 1842. In 1861, he was elected to the first Confederate Congress. In 1866, he served on the Union National Convention and in 1868 was elected county commissioner. He served numerous sessions as justice of the pleas court. His first wife was Mary Jones Arrington, and his second was Kate Wimberly. Arrington had nine children, six of which lived to adulthood. He died in 1872 and is buried on the homeplace in Hilliardston. (Marrow.)

Born in 1844 to one of the founding families of Nash County, Benjamin Hickman joined the Confederate army at the age of 17. After the war, he returned home to study law. After passing the bar, Bunn practiced law for 40 years. He led the campaign to get Rocky Mount incorporated in 1867 and became the first mayor. He was elected to Congress in 1888. Bunn married Harriet Philips of Edgecombe County, and they had nine children at their home in Benvenue, where Bunn died in 1907. (NCDAH.)

Dr. Wimberly was born in 1862 and attended the University of Maryland Medical School. He began his practice in Edgecombe County, but moved to Rocky Mount in 1886 and practiced medicine until his death in 1941. Wimberly was married to Mary Bunn. Other Nash County physicians included Dr. William Whitehead and his son, Dr. Joseph Whitehead; Dr. Cornelius Braswell and his son, Dr. James C. Braswell; and Dr. Richard Speight of Tarboro and his three sons, Richard Speight Jr., Joseph Powell Speight, and James Amble Speight. (Barringer.)

In 1970, the charter members of the Rocky Mount Kiwanis Club celebrated the organization's 50th anniversary. The members, from left to right, are as follows: F.E. Winslow, J.B. Bulluck, Josh L. Horne, K.D. Battle, and M.P. Dawson. (Barringer.)

Tom Stith began Boy Scout Troop # 161 in 1919. A Rocky Mount park located on the corner of Spruce Street and Atlantic Avenue is named after him. (Barringer.)

Martha Westray Battle Boyce came from a long line of Nash and Edgecombe County residents. Her great-great-grandfather was Elisha Battle, who settled the area in the 1740s. Her great-grandfather Turner Westray Battle was captain of the Confederate Guards, a local company in the Civil War. Her grandfather Jacob Battle was a state senator and superior court judge. In 1942, she volunteered to join the army. By the end of the war, she would be the director of the WACs, the highest woman officer in the U.S. Army. She died in 1972. (Barringer.)

A native of Halifax County, Maurice V. Barnhill graduated from the U.N.C. School of Law and began practicing law in Rocky Mount in 1910. Barnhill practiced law for 27 years. He was a superior court judge from 1924 to 1937, when he was appointed to the state supreme court. In 1951, he became the chief justice of the North Carolina Supreme Court. Barnhill married Rebecca Cooper of Rocky Mount, and they had two children. Barnhill died in 1963. (Barringer.)

Rocky Mount was the home of another Supreme Court justice, Susie Sharp. When Susie was in high school, her family moved to Reidsville, where she finished school. She attended U.N.C. and passed the bar. She was the first woman in the United States to be appointed to a state supreme court and in 1974 became the first woman to be chief justice of a state court in the United States. (Barringer.)

Roger Atkinson Pryor Cooley was the father of Congressman Cooley. He and his wife, Harriet, had five children before Roger died unexpectedly in 1906. (NCDAH.)

Harriet Davis Cooley, the wife of Roger Cooley and mother of Harold Cooley, died in 1913, leaving her five young children to raise themselves. (NCDAH.)

Harold, the son of Roger and Harriet Cooley, was born in 1897 in Nashville. A student at U.N.C.-Chapel Hill, Cooley applied for the bar before he finished law school. He passed and was licensed on his 21st birthday. In 1934, he was elected to Congress, where he served for 17 consecutive terms. In 1966, Cooley would be challenged and defeated for his congressional seat by a young Republican, Jim Gardner. Cooley married Madeline Strickland, and they raised two children in the Cooley mansion in Nashville. Cooley (center) is here with Vice-President Barkley (left) on a tour of North Carolina farms. (NCDAH.)

Born in 1926, Itimous "Tim" Valentine graduated from The Citadel with a degree in political science after serving two years in the U.S. Army Corp during WW II. He then attended U.N.C. Law School. Valentine was elected to the North Carolina Legislature from 1954 to 1960. During much of the 1960s, he worked as an advisor to Governor Moore. In 1982, Valentine was elected to Congress and he served through 1994. Valentine is married to Barbara Reynolds, and they have seven children. (Valentine.)

Cara Bunn Sessoms was one of the most influential African-American teachers in the history of Nash County. Born in the 1880s, Cara attended a private school in 1890 established by Mrs. Rachel Thomas. For her love and dedication to education and to her race, Cara became one of the first African-American teachers in the Rocky Mount school system. She was honored at Booker T. Washington High School for her contributions to education. (Barringer.)

The son of Police Sergeant Z.H. Wheeless, Dan Wheeless was in a Korean prison camp for 28 months before he was released in August 1953. Captured in 1951, just north of the 38th parallel, he was kept in a prison just south of the Chinese border. He arrived at Raleigh Airport on September 6 greeted by friends and family. (Barringer.)

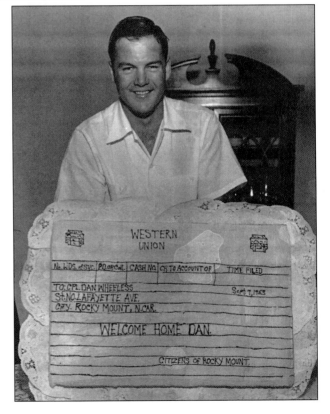

In 1892, Paul B. Kyser came to Rocky Mount and established a drugstore. His wife, Emily, was the first woman pharmacist registered in North Carolina. In 1906, they had a son, James Kern, who was better known as "Kay." Kay became world renowned, and in WW II, he entertained troops in Europe. After a successful and demanding musical career, he returned to Chapel Hill in 1951, where he helped establish the public television station. Kay married Georgia Caroll, and they had three children. He died in 1985 and is buried in Chapel Hill. (Barringer.)

Jazz musician Thelonious Sphere Monk was born in this house in Rocky Mount in 1917. His parents, Thelonious and Barbara Batts Monk, moved to New York while Monk was a child. By the late 1930s, Monk was playing clubs around New York, becoming an innovator of music and one of the founders of "Bebop" jazz. Composer of over 70 works, Monk died in New Jersey in 1982. His son, Thelonious Jr., has returned to Rocky Mount for special concerts to commemorate his father in the Harambee Festivals. (RMECDC.)

In 1944, O.L. "Buggs" Barringer opened a photography studio on Western Avenue, and it became known throughout the state. Buggs was known for portraits and commercial photography, but he also loved to take news and spot photos. In 1977, Buggs and his wife, Dot, along with Lela Chesson, published the first photographic record of Rocky Mount. Buggs continued to operate his studio until the 1990s. In 1997, David Chicelli acquired the studio after the death of Buggs and relocated the studio to a larger store on Church Street. (Barringer.)

In 1946, Buggs won a photographic press award with this photo of a newsstand and its young customer. (Barringer.)